THE ICE STORM

THE ICE STORM
John Ashbery

HANUMAN EDITIONS

"The Ice Storm" was first published in *Temblor #5*, and subsequently in *April Galleons*, both in 1987, as well as the Library of American collection *Collected poems 1956-1987* (2008). It was published by Hanuman Books in 1987.

© 1987, 2023, the Estate of John Ashbery

Cover photo: John Ashbery, *After a Summer Downpour* © 1971, 2023 by Gerard Malanga

ISBN 979-8-9893780-1-2

Printed in the UK.
Typeset in Arnhem Fine, with Eksell and Caslon No540 Swash D.

Hanuman Editions
London & Seattle
hanumaneditions.com

The Ice Storm

isn't really a storm
of course because
unlike most storms
it isn't one till it's
over and people go
outside and say will

you look at that. And
by then it's of course
starting to collapse.
Diamond rubble, all
galled glitter, heaps
of this and that in
corners and beside
posts where the draft
has left them—are

you sure it's this you
were waiting for
while the storm—the
real one—pressed it
all into the earth to
emphasize a point that
melts away as fast as
another idea enters
the chain of them

in the conversation
about earth and sky
and woods and how
you should be good
to your parents and
not cheat at cards.
The summer's almost
over it seems to say.
Did I say summer I

meant to say winter it seems to say. You know when nature really has to claw like this to get her effects that something's not ripe or nice, i.e. the winter, our favorite of seasons, the one

that goes by quickest
although you almost
never hear anyone
say, I wonder where
the winter has gone.
But anyone engaged
in the business of
swapping purity for
depth will understand

what I mean. So we all
eyeball it, agog, for a
while. And soon our
attention is trapped
by news from the
cities, by what comes
over the wireless—
heated, and alight.
How natural then

to retreat into what
we have been doing,
trying to capture the
old songs, the idiot
games whose rules
have been forgotten.
"Here we go looby,
looby." And the exact
name of the season

that strings like a
needle made of frozen
mercury falls through
the infinitesimal hole
in our consciousness,
to plummet hundreds
of leagues into the
sea and vanish in a
perpetual descent

toward the ocean
floor, whatever and
wherever that may be,
and the great undersea
storms and cataclysms
will leave no trace
on the seismographs
each of us wears in the
guise of a head.

To do that, though—get up and out from under the pile of required reading such as obituary notices of the near-great—"He first gained employment as a schoolmaster

in his native
Northamptonshire.
Of his legendary wit,
no trace remains"—
is something that
will go unthought
of until another day.
Sure we know that
the government and

the president want it.
But we know just as
surely that until the
actual slippage occurs,
the actual moment
of uncertainty by
two or more of the
plates or tectons
that comprise the

earth's crust, nobody is ever going to be moved to the point of action. You might as well call it a night, go to sleep under a bushel basket. For the probability of that moment occurring is next to nil. I mean it will probably never happen and if it does, chances are we won't be around to witness any of it.

The warp, the woof. (What actually, are they? Never mind,

save that for another
time when the old
guy's gotten a bit
more soused.) Or the
actual strings of words
on the two pages of
a book, like I was
reading this novel,
I think the author

was associated with the Kailyard School. What's that? Wait, though—I think I know. What I really want to know is how will this affect me, make me better in the future? Maybe

make me a better
conversationalist?
But nobody ever talks
about the Kailyard
School, at least not
at the dinner parties
I go to. What, then?
Will it be that having
accomplished the

tale of this reading there will only be about seven million more books to go, and that's something, or is it more the act of reading something, of being communicated to by an author and

thus having one's
ideas displaced like
the water that pebbles
placed by the stork's
beak slowly force out
of the beaker—*beaker?*
Do you suppose? No
I wasn't suggesting
anything like that.

I want to cut out of this conversation or discourse. Why? Because it doesn't seem to be leading anywhere. Besides it could compromise me when the results become known, and

by results I mean the
slightest ripple that
occurs as when the
breeze lifts a corner
of the vast torpid
flag dropping at its
standard, like the
hairline crack in the
milkwhite china of

the sky, that indicates something is off, something less likable than the situation a few moments before has assumed its place in the pre-ordained hierarchy of things. Something like the

leaves of this plan
with its veins that
almost look parallel
though they are
radiating from its
center of course.

It's odd about things
like plants. Today I
found a rose in full

bloom in the wreck
of the garden, all
the living color and
sentience but also
the sententiousness
drained out of it.
What remained was
like a small flower
in the woods, too

pale and sickly to
notice. No, sickly isn't
the right word, the
thing was normal
and healthy by its
own standards, and
thriving merrily
along its allotted path
toward death. Only we

hold it up to some real and abject notion of what a living organism ought to be and paint it a scarecrow, that frightens birds away (presumably) but isn't able to frighten itself away. Oh, no, it's far too clever for that! But our flower, the one we saw, really had no need of us to justify its blooming where it did. So we ought to think about our own position on the path. Will it ever

be anything more
than that of pebble?
I wonder. And they
scratch some of them
feverishly, at whatever
meaning it might
supposed to yield up,
of course expiring as it
does so. But our rose

gains its distinction
just by being stuck
there as though by
the distracted hand
of a caterer putting
the finishing touch
on some grand floral
dis-play for a society
wedding that will be

over in a few minutes, a season not of its own naming. Why appear at a time when the idea of a flower can make no sense, not even in its isolation? It's just that nature forces us into odd positions and then sits back to hear us squawk but may, indeed, derive no comfort or pleasure from this. And as I lifted it gently I saw that it was doing what it was supposed to do—miming freshness tracked by pathos. What more do you want? it seemed to say. Leave me in this desert. . .

As I straighten my footsteps to accommodate the

narrow path that has
been chosen for me I
begin to cringe at the
notion that I can never
be accommodated
here, no not like
the rose blooming
grotesquely out of
season even, but must

always consider the sharp edges of the slender stones set upright in the earth, to be my guide and commentator, on this path. I was talking to some of the others about it. But if it

didn't matter then,
it matters now, now
that I begin to get
my bearings in this
gloom and see how I
could improve on the
distraught situation
all around me, in
the darkness and

tarnished earth. Yet who will save me from myself if they can't? I can't, certainly, yet I tell myself it all seems like fun and will work out in the end. I expect I will be asked a question I can answer

and then be handed
a big prize. They're
working on it.

So the sunlit snow
slips daintily down
the waterway to the
open sea, the car
with its driver along
the looping drives

that bisect suburbs and then flatten out through town that are partly rural though with some suburban characteristics. Only I stay here alone, waiting for it to reach the point of cohesion.

Or maybe I'm not
alone, maybe there are
other me's, but in that
case the cohesion may
have happened already
and we are no wiser
for it, despite being
positioned around to
comment on it like

statues around a view.
The dry illumination
that results from
that will not help us,
it will always be as
though we had never
happened, ornaments
on a structure whose
mass remains invisible

or illegible.

   October 28.
Three more days till
November. I expect
this to happen in a
soft ex-
plosion of powdery
light, dull and
nameless, though not

without a sense of humor in its crevices, where darkness still lives and enjoys going about its business. There are too many stones to make it interesting to hobble from one to an-

other. Perhaps in a few
days… Maybe by the time
I finish the course I
am taking, if sirens
don't dislodge me
from this pure and
valid niche. I feel that
this season is being

pulled over my head
like a dress, difficult
to spot the dirt in
its mauve and brick
traceries. I am being
taken out into the
country. Trees flash
past. All is perhaps for
the best then since I

am going, and they are
going with us, with us
as we go. The past is
only a pond.
The present is a lake
of grass. Between your
two futures, yours and
his, numbing twigs
chart the pattern of

lifeless chatter in shut-
down night, starstruck
the magnitudes that
would make us theirs,
too cold to matter
to themselves, let us
be off anywhere, to
Alaska, to Arizona.
I am fishing for

compliments. The afternoon lasts forever.

Hanuman Editions is designed, edited, and published by Shruti Belliappa and Joshua Rothes, in friendship, with gratitude to Raymond Foye and Francesco Clemente, for these treasures and blessings.